Other books by Exley:
Golf Quotations
Golf Jokes
Golf Score Book

The Golfer's Address Book
The Fanatics Guide to Golf
The Crazy World of Golf

Published simultaneously in 1993 by Exley Publications
in Great Britain, and Exley Giftbooks in the USA.
Second printing 1994.
Selection and arrangement © Helen Exley 1993.
ISBN 1-85015-442-2

Edited by Helen Exley.
Designed by Pinpoint Design.
Picture research by P. A. Goldberg and J. M. Clift/Image
Select, London.
Typeset by Delta, Watford.
Printed at Grafo S.A., Bilbao, Spain.

Exley Publications Ltd, 16 Chalk Hill, Watford, Herts WD1 4BN, U.K.
Exley Giftbooks, 232 Madison Avenue, Suite 1206, NY 10016, USA.

The Publishers wish to thank Rosenstiel's Widow and Son Ltd. and The
Burlington Gallery for their help in providing pictures for this book.
Cover: Exley Publications; Sara Fabian Baddiel, Golfiana, Grays in the Mews,
B10 Davies Mews, London W1, tel: 071-408-1239: title page and pages 7, 8, 11,
12, 14, 16, 19, 20, 22, 27, 30, 32, 34, 37, 41, 42, 47, 48, 50, 53, 55, 57, 58, 61;
Bridgeman Art Library: pages 29, 38, 45; Eaton Gallery, London: page 29;
Illustrated London News: page 25; © John Sutton "The fifth tee St. Andrew's
1921": page 29.

GOLF

A CELEBRATION IN WORDS AND PAINTINGS

SELECTED BY
HELEN EXLEY

EXLEY
NEW YORK • WATFORD, UK

THE GREATEST GAME OF ALL

❖

Beyond the fact that it is a limitless arena for the full play of human nature, there is no sure accounting for golf's fascination. Obviously yet mysteriously, it furnishes its devotees with an intense, many-sided, and abiding pleasure unlike that which any other form of recreation affords. Perhaps it is, as Andrew Carnegie once claimed, an "indispensable adjunct of high civilization." Perhaps it is nothing more than the best game man has ever devised.

HERBERT WARREN WIND,
FROM *"THE COMPLETE GOLFER"*

❖

When I look on my life and try to decide out of what I have got most actual pleasure, I have no doubt at all in saying that I have got more out of golf than anything else.

LORD BRABAZON OF TARA, 1956

❖

Golf is not a relaxation, golf is everything, golf is a philosophy, it's a religion, absolutely, I mean really absolutely.

SIR BOB REID

❖

Around the first tee old comrades are assembling. Jaunty youth mingles with seasoned manhood. Jocund natures measure drivers with sedate temperaments. Exultant enthusiasts cross mid-irons with dismal pessimists.... So gathers the clan at the reveille of springtime, trailing in and out of locker-house, swarming in groups like so many bees, only to fly apart before fully settling. Greetings are bowed, and smiled, and waved, and gripped. Faces you have not seen all winter pop up again. Embers of carried-over friendships are fanned into flames of renewed encounters. Memories, like a scarlet thread running through the frosted winter months, bind old rivalries to new challenges. Cares are tossed to the wind. Tense nerves are relaxed. Crow's-feet are ironed out, cheeks glow, and eyes brim with anticipation. Your hibernated blood awakens as your hand grips the club, and once more you are alive and in love with life in the open.

CHARLES W. MOORE,
FROM *"THE MENTAL SIDE OF GOLF"*

HOOKED!

❖

From the moment one of the Philistines essays a stroke, and by accident makes a fair drive from a tee, his conversion is assured, he has ... learned "to endure, then pity, then embrace" ... henceforth he will strive persistently, in season and out of season, to show "the golf that is in him"; he will regret the neglected opportunities of his youth, and the disease which has no microbe and no cure is chronic and seated on him for life. Henceforward, he will adapt the motto of the Hittormissit Club: "Drive it if you can, club it if you will, kick it if you must."

"SCRIBNER'S MAGAZINE"

Golf is essentially an exercise in masochism conducted out of doors; it induces a sense of kinship in its victims ... but it is, at bottom, an elaborate and addictive rite calculated to drive them crazy.

PAUL O'NEIL

For the golfer, Nature loses her significance. Larks, the casts of worms, the buzzing of bees, and even children are hateful to him....Rain comes to be regarded solely in its relation to the putting greens; the daisy is detested, botanical specimens are but "hazards", twigs "break clubs." Winds cease to be east, south, west, or north. They are ahead, behind, or sideways, and the sky is bright or dark, according to the state of the game.

SIR W. G. SIMPSON,
FROM *"THE ART OF GOLF"*

The duffer is puzzled at the extraordinary fascination which his new-found pass-time exercises over him. He came to scoff; he remains to play...

ARNOLD HAULTAIN

THE GOLF BUG

We own that at first sight it is difficult for the uninitiated looker-on to sympathise with the evident enthusiasm of the players. There does not seem to be anything very stimulating in grinding round a barren stretch of ground, impelling a gutta-percha ball before you, striving to land it in a succession of small holes in fewer strokes than your companion and opponent. But as to the reality of the excitement, you are soon compelled to take that for granted. You see gentlemen of all ages, often of the

most self-indulgent or sedentary habits, turning out in every kind of weather, persevering to the dusk of a winter day, in spite of bitter wind and driving showers; or dragging about their cumbrous weight of flesh in hot defiance of the most sultry summer temperature. The truth is that, appearances not withstanding, experience proves it to be one of the most fascinating of pursuits...

FROM *"THE TIMES OF LONDON", 1874*

The golf bug has many insidious symptoms and manifests itself by filling your head with dreams of greatness - "If I'd only started younger, I'd be another Faldo..." It also covers your hands with calluses and fills your house with accoutrements you'd never heard of last year, and will probably never need next year. The bug even affects the way you celebrate Christmas, miraculously changing all Yuletide presents from ties, hankies and socks to balls, tees, hip flasks, all kinds of golfing gimmicks.... The bug bit me in 1977 and I have not been the same man since.

TOM O'CONNOR,
FROM *"FROM THE WOOD TO THE TEES"*

Golf is more exacting than racing, cards, speculation or matrimony. Golf gives no margin: either you win or you fail. You cannot hedge; you cannot bluff; you cannot give a stop-order; you cannot jilt. One chance is given you, and you hit or miss. There is nothing more rigid in life. And it is this ultra and extreme rigidity that makes golf so intensely interesting.

······

Eighteen dramas, some tragical, some farcical, in every round; and in every round protagonist and deuteragonist constantly interchanging parts. No wonder the ardent golfer does not tire of his links, any more than the ardent musician tires of his notes. What theatre-goer enjoys such plays? And what staged plays have such a human interest in them? And, best of all, they are acted in the open air, amid delightful scenery, with the assurance of healthy exercise and pleasant companionship.

ARNOLD HAULTAIN

A DIVINE COMEDY!

The humour of golf is a divine comedy in the deepest sense. Like all sources of laughter it lies in contrast and paradox; in the thought of otherwise grave men gravely devoting hours and money to a technique which so often they, apparently alone, do not know they can never master. The solemnity of their eternal failure is vastly comic. The perpetualness of their hope is nobly humorous.

R. C. ROBERTSON-GLASGOW

That there is some secret which, if discovered, would make our driving infallible is a belief which dies hard. Nostrum after nostrum is tried day after day. Hope is quickly followed by a despairing desire to break the whole set or spitefully to present them to a friend, so that he too may suffer.

SIR W. G. SIMPSON

WHAT RELAXATION?

A man named Dick Brooks wrote about golf. He claims that a man, standing up to a ball armed only with a club, undergoes shortness of breath, tightness in the chest, curling of the toes, back ache, clenched teeth, locked knees, muscle spasms and paralysis.

In sum, he's ready to hit.

JIM BISHOP,
FROM *"A TRIBUTE TO GOLF"*

·•●●•·

The hacker dreams of relaxing as though, in golf, lassitude will cut 10 strokes from his game. *Au contraire.* He who relaxes is a ruptured pigeon. Good players find that a mixture of equal parts of tension, hatred, and self-loathing insure a good round.

It is not only permissible, but desirable, to despise the course, the ball, wives, children, and weather and the score.

JIM BISHOP,
FROM *"A TRIBUTE TO GOLF"*

Men of dignity and business acumen when sailing through the corridors of power with a flock of underlings and yes-men in their wake become semi-paralytic when overcome by first tee nerves.

BEN WRIGHT

❖

FRIENDSHIP

❖

The game is so fostered by companionship and wrapped about with the joys of friendship, that he who has his soul's friend for his golfing mate is on fortune's cap the very button.

With such company, when the November wind streams down the course, whipping out our little clouds of breath into streamers, we can stride over our 18 holes with the keen joy of living that comes at intervals to the tired worker.

And then, oh! weary soul, what joys await the faithful! The putting off of mud-caked shoes, the brisk plunge or shower-bath, and the warm glow thereafter; the immaculate shirt-front that crackles at your touch, the glad joy of dinner and the utter relaxation of content, "with just a wee drappie of guid Scotch to follow".

"SCRIBNER'S MAGAZINE", **1895**

No other game or sport exercises anything like such power of fascination upon its people as this ... the golfer will and must always golf, and never less but more while strength permits. Men who go down to the sea in ships take golf clubs with them; I have known golfers carry their materials into deserts, and one of the greatest and noblest explorers the world has known took them with him to one far end of the earth. Surely this is a very remarkable thing, a feature of life that is strange as it is strong, and it is not nonsense to suggest that this is no ordinary game and cannot be considered as a game like others. Somewhere in a mysterious way it touches the springs of life, makes emotions shake. It grips; it twitches at the senses... It has become the Great Mystery. Wonder and awe are thick about it. People who were innocent and have turned to golf do not give a reason why; they are silent to the questioner.

HENRY LEACH

Caddies are a breed of their own. If you shoot sixty-six, they say, "Man, we shot sixty-six!" But go out and shoot seventy-seven, and they say, "Hell, he shot seventy-seven!"

LEE TREVINO

From men who have adopted carrying as a trade, the golfer is entitled to expect the highest standard of efficiency. If he carries for you regularly, he ought to know what club you intend to take, and to give it without being asked. When you are in doubt about how to play your shot, he ought to confirm you in the opinion you have formed regarding it. He must never show the just contempt he has for your game.

SIR WALTER SIMPSON

Speak gruffly to your caddie boy,
And kick him when he sneezes;
Your peace of mind he'll else destroy
With grunts and groans and wheezes.

GERALD BATCHELOR

There are three classes of people who are entitled to refer to themselves as "We." They are Kings, Editors, and Caddies.

GERALD BATCHELOR

OUT IN THE OPEN

❖

And this drama of the emotions of the individual is played always in the most perfect setting for such a simple human play - the sea and green fields and plain earth, and the simplest tools to move a little white ball, not along marked lines or within narrow limits or in protected arenas, but anywhere along that green grass, over the hills and through the valleys and across the streams and rushing rivers, while the wind blows now this way and then that, and the rain pours. All the time the golfer pursues the little ball, alone with nature and his human adversary. Here he is released from all the conventionalities of mind.... The primitive instincts are in command: they have the fields and the sea for harmony in the scene, and the golfer is away from all the intricacies of the twentieth century, and is the simple man and the hopeful man.

HENRY LEACH

St. Andrews! they say that thy glories are gone,
That thy streets are deserted, thy castles o'er thrown:
If thy glories *be* gone, they are only, methinks,
As it were, by enchantment, transferr'd to thy Links.
Though thy streets be not now, as of yore, full of
prelates,
Of abbots and monks, and of hot-headed zealots,
Let none judge us rashly, or blame us as scoffers,
When we say that instead there are Links full of Golfers,
With more of good heart and good feeling among them
Than the abbots, the monks, and the zealots who sung
them:
We have red coats and bonnets, we've putters and clubs;
The green has its bunkers, its hazards, and rubs;
At the long hole across we have biscuits and beer,
And the Hebes we sell it give zest to the cheer:
If this makes not up for the pomp and the splendour
Of mitres, and murders, and mass - we'll surrender;
If Golfers and caddies be not better neighbours
Than abbots and soldiers with crosses and sabres,
Let such fancies remain with the fool who so thinks,
While we toast old St. Andrews, its Golfers and Links.

GEORGE FULLERTON CARNEGIE, FROM *"GOLFIANA"* (1833)

If the golfer could overcome his mental hazards, he would have an easier game than if all the ponds and streams were dry, and all the traps filled, and all the bunkers cut down!

CHARLES W. MOORE,
FROM *"THE MENTAL SIDE OF GOLF"*

There is no other game that strips the soul
so naked.

H. G. HUTCHINSON

Golf allows us to build and transform personal
character. Out of the surge of competitive spirit
rise the gamut of our highest and lowest
instincts. It is such a naked occupation. We are
exposed far beyond the limits we normally
allow. The lighter and darker sides of our
persona or being may be exhibited within a
single hole.

TOM STEWART,
FROM *"A TRIBUTE TO GOLF"*

The enthusiast's ... sense of the ultimate
purpose and the true proportions of his
existence is unruffled ... his soul is so wrapped
in the harmony of earth and sky and the glory
of the game that no buffets of fortune can come
at him.

"SCRIBNER'S MAGAZINE"

DEMANDING EVERYTHING

❖

It is a game in which the whole temperamental strength of one side is hurled against the strength of the other, and the two human natures are pressing bitterly and relentlessly against each other from the first moment of the game to the last. It is the whole person, mind and body. That is the meaning of the temperamental factor in golf, and that is why a great match at golf is great indeed.

HENRY LEACH

Golf, to the man or woman who regards it simply as a game, will remain for ever insoluble and an enigma, and it will retain its greatness because it contains something that lifts it higher than that of a mere pastime.

J. H. TAYLOR

AWAY FROM IT ALL

With a fine sea view, and a clear course in front, the golfer should find no difficulty in dismissing all worries from the mind, and regarding golf, even it may be indifferent golf, as the true and adequate end of existence. No inconvenient reminiscences of the ordinary workaday world, no intervals of weariness or monotony interrupt the pleasures of the game.

EARL BALFOUR

❖

Golf's predictable structure is both comforting and relaxing. We can almost predict the exact words our playing partners will use to set up the game on the first tee. This predictability provides a safe harbor for a few hours to avoid some of the storms of the everyday world. Golf absorbs our minds, and the mental tribulations of our lives are put on hold as we wrestle with errant drives, pulled approach shots and missed putts.

DR. RICHARD H. COOP, 1989

❖

The golfer...is never old until he is decrepit. So long as Providence allows him the use of two legs active enough to carry him round the green, and two arms supple enough to take a "half swing", there is no reason why his enjoyment in the game need be seriously diminished.

ARTHUR BALFOUR

I was shown one particular set of golfers, the youngest of whom was turned four-score. They were all gentlemen of independent fortunes, who had amused themselves with this pastime for the best part of a century, without having ever felt the least alarm from sickness or disgust; and they never went to bed without having each the best part of a gallon of claret in his belly. Such uninterrupted exercise, co-operating with the keen air from the sea, must, without all doubt, keep the appetite always on edge, and steel the constitution against all the common attacks of distemper.

TOBIAS SMOLLETT (1721-1771),
FROM "HUMPHREY CLINKER"

It can be begun as soon as you walk, and once begun it is continued as long as you can see.

SCRIBNER MAGAZINE

❖

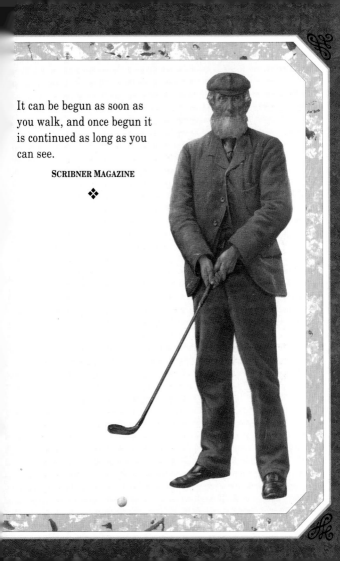

33.—MacFoozle.
Chief of the Clan.

MACFOOZLE

In golf almost everything the player does falls into
three categories - slightly wrong, wrong and disastrous.
The player who executes good shots is referred to
scornfully as a hustler. It is the only game in
which a degree of excellence elicits contempt...

JIM BISHOP

Golf is the hardest game in the world.
There's no way you can ever get it. Just when you
think you do, the game jumps up and puts you
into your place.

BEN CRENSHAW

Is there any other game in which the player is so
constantly wondering what is the matter with him and
so regularly finding a cure which he believes will heal
him for ever, only to suffer a dreadful relapse next day?

BERNARD DARWIN

Never hurry, never worry and always remember to smell the flowers along the way.

WALTER HAGEN

Half the battle of golf consists in taking it easy. Irritation over a bad shot, anxiety over a bunker in front of you, and especially the effort to drive against a strong wind, may tempt you to hurry your swing. If you give in to the impulse, the result will be bad, and the habit will grow on you.

"OUTING"

The great mistake that most make is thinking ahead of the stroke, not with it. Never mind where the ball is going: first of all it has to be hit in the right way before it will go in the right place. Think of that side of the matter.

GLENNA COLLETT VANE,
FROM *"THE AMERICAN GOLFER"*

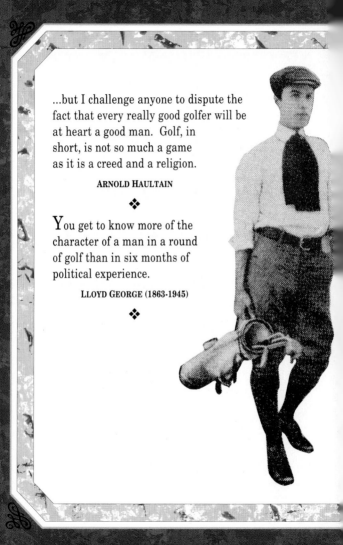

...but I challenge anyone to dispute the fact that every really good golfer will be at heart a good man. Golf, in short, is not so much a game as it is a creed and a religion.

ARNOLD HAULTAIN

❖

You get to know more of the character of a man in a round of golf than in six months of political experience.

LLOYD GEORGE (1863-1945)

❖

When you reflect on the combination of characteristics that golf demands of those who would presume to play it, it is not surprising that golf has never had a truly great player who was not also a person of extraordinary character.

FRANK D. *"SANDY"* TUTMAN, JR

Good sportsmanship is the essence of golf, and no one exemplified that more than Bobby Jones. In the 1925 U.S. Open, Jones's ball moved when he addressed it. No one else had seen it move, so Jones called the penalty on himself. That penalty ended up costing him the championship.

"There's only one way to play the game," he said when later asked about it. "You might as well praise a man for not robbing a bank as to praise him for playing by the rules."

FROM *"GOLF THE LORE OF THE LINKS"*

To some minds the great field which golf opens up for exaggeration is its chief attraction.

SIR W. G. SIMPSON

If you pick up a golfer and hold it close to your ear, like a conch shell, and listen, you will hear an alibi.

FRED BECK

Long experience upon the links teaches one to be genially tolerant of the mathematical miscalculations of others. It is a strange thing that men who invariably add up a bridge score correctly - Wall Street magnates, captains of industry, masters of finance who can tell offhand the profit they have made on 460 Canadian Pacific ordinary shares when the stock rises three points - often display a lamentable incapacity for estimating the exact number of times they have struck a golf ball between the tee and the green. Persons of unblemished reputation and scrupulous integrity will entirely forget whether they took three or four strokes to get out of a bunker; the fact that their first drive went out of bounds, and that they were forced to play a second shot from the tee, escapes their memory in a way that non-golfers might deem incredible.

HARRY GRAHAM,
FROM *"THE COMPLETE SPORTSMAN"*

Golf is a game in which you yell fore, shoot six, and write down five.

PAUL HARVEY

YOUR OWN WORST ENEMY

Golf is not a wrestle with Bogey; it is not a struggle with your mortal foe; it is a physiological, psychological, and moral fight with yourself; it is a test of mastery over self; and the ultimate and irreducible element of the game is to determine which of the players is the more worthy combatant.

ARNOLD HAULTAIN

The person I fear most in the last two rounds is myself.

TOM WATSON

In a gin'ral way, all I can say about it is that it's a kind iv game iv ball that ye play with ye'er own worst inimy, which is ye'ersilf.

FINLEY PETER DUNNE (1867-1936),
QUOTED IN *"GOLF'S GOLDEN GRIND"* **BY AL BARKOW**

In almost all other games you pit yourself against a mortal foe; in golf it is yourself against the world: no human being stays your progress as you drive your ball over the face of the globe.

ARNOLD HAULTAIN,
FROM *"THE MYSTERY OF GOLF"*

❖

C. W. FAULKNER

Golf: Putting

"!?#*!"

The most exquisitely satisfying act in the world of golf is that of throwing a club. The full backswing, the delayed wrist action, the flowing follow-through, followed by that unique whirring sound, reminiscent only of a passing flock of starlings, are without parallel in sport.

HENRY LONGHURST

To the language with which every golf course is strewn, differing more in form than in substance, from the "Tut, tut, tut" of the ecclesiastic to the more sulphurous exclamation of the layman, the divine quality of forgiveness must be extended.

"SCRIBNER'S MAGAZINE", **1895**

The niblick, with its heavy head of iron, is a capital club for knocking down solicitors.

ANON

A VARIETY OF TROUBLES!

No golfer has ever been forced to say to himself with tears, "There are no more links to conquer".

JOHN L. LOW

A Scotch proverb says, "He who plays with a thistle must expect to get pricked", and he who plays golf must expect to get into trouble. Indeed, a golfer's life is one continuous series of problems: "How to get out of trouble".

Trouble he will have, willy-nilly. This may at the first blush seem a somewhat dispiriting view to take of so fascinating a game, but it is the very variety of the points of the game, ever occurring yet scarcely ever duplicated, that gives it its unique position. It is this that renders it so exhilarating to the devotee, both mentally and physically.

"OUTING"

The golfer has more enemies than any other athlete. He has fourteen clubs in his bag, all of them different; eighteen holes to play, all of them different, every week; and all around him are sand, trees, grass, water, wind, and 143 other players.

DAN JENKINS

Golf may be, and is, used by people of every colour, race, creed and temperament, in every climate and all the year round. No recreation, apart from the simplest contests of the river and field, has been so universal since the world began, with the single exception of chess. And wherever and whenever it is played, it extends its benign influence towards the promotion of fast friendship among the players. There is no freemasonry like the freemasonry of golf. To its temples in every land are always welcomed the faithful and earnest craftsman from where'er he came, and he is passed on the signs of the bag and the stance and the little pimpled ball. For it is one of the articles of belief that no man can be a good and enthusiastic golfer of experience and at the same time a thoroughly bad fellow, for at the outset of his career the bad fellow would never be happy in his game.... Thus has our happy game of golf wound a bright cordon round the world, and so does she play her part in the great evolution of general contentment.

HENRY LEACH

FOR HEALTH AND A LONG LIFE

If you were assured that without imbibing any new-fangled religion and regardless of all the new dietists and doctors, you could not only add twenty years to the normal span of life, but secure in the present at least one good day out of seven by the simple process of swinging a golf club, would you not rush out to the nearest links and begin to take lessons?

"OUTING"

There is no shape nor size of body, no awkwardness nor ungainliness, which puts good golf beyond one's reach. There are good golfers with spectacles, with one eye, with one leg, even with one arm. None but the absolutely blind need despair. It is not the youthful tyro alone who has cause to hope. Beginners in middle age have become great, and, more wonderful still, after years of patient duffering, there may be a rift in the clouds.

Some pet vice which has been clung to as a virtue may be abandoned, and the fifth-class player burst upon the world as a medal winner. In golf, whilst there is life there is hope.

SIR W. G. SIMPSON

❖

Like life, golf can be humbling. However, little good comes from brooding about mistakes we've made. The next shot, in golf or in life, is the big one.

GRANTLAND RICE

...but every moderately good golfer, on the morning of the medal day, may lie abed and count up a perfect score for himself. He easily recalls how at different times and how often he has done each hole in par figures. Why not this day, and all the holes consecutively? It seems so easy.... Every competitor who is awake soon enough sees the necessity for preparing a speech against the contingency of the medal being presented to him in the evening. Nor is any one much crushed when all is over, and he has not won. If he does well, it was but that putt, that bad lie, that bunker. If his score is bad, what of it? Even the best are off their game occasionally.
Next time it will be different.

SIR WALTER SIMPSON, 1887

TIMES REMEMBERED

❖

You cannot be around golf without absorbing a
sense of its history, its richness. Golf is legends
and lore, great images and greater vision.
It's the sense of awe you get when someone
so much as mentions Bobby Jones. It's the

overwhelming feeling of wonder and tradition that is there, walking alongside you, when you step to the first tee at St. Andrews, or Augusta, or Pebble Beach.

ARNOLD PALMER

I think not only of quiet corners of many courses, but of many fields where the grass was so long that almost every stroke involved a search; I think of a mountain top in Wales and a plain in Macedonia; of innumerable floors on which I have tried to hit the table legs; I recall rain and wind and mud and the shades of evening falling, so that the lights came twinkling out in the houses round the links, and the ball's destiny was a matter of pure conjecture. Remembering all these things, I can say that I may have been an unprofitable practiser, but that at any rate I have been a happy one.

BERNARD DARWIN,
FROM *"GOLF"*

At the End of the Year

———— ❖ ————

How much does it mean to us, does a year of golf! In the last few moments of the year that you give up to golfing thought and reverie as you sit by the cheerful fire and perhaps, according to the old fancy, toy on the hearthrug for a while with the putter that you hold at convenience in the corner and the memento ball that you preserve upon the mantelpiece - at such time make a pleasant reflection upon all the joy and the gladness, and the health and the adventure, and the glorious rivalry and the close comradeship that have been crowded into this short space of time! Above all, think how much nearer in most blessed friendship has this year of golf drawn you to those who are most after your own heart! There is no habit of man that can do more than golf towards such an end as this, and it is in his abundance of the best friends that a man lives most happily....

HENRY LEACH, FROM *"IN PRAISE OF GOLF"*